A GIFT TO AMERICA

by
Jane Mylum Gardner

Illustrated by Susan Bolduc

Grateful acknowledgement is made to
The Museum of the City of New York,
to the New York Historical Society,
and to the New York Public Library for pictorial references.

Gardner Publishing, Inc.

ISBN 0-9617183-0-7

A Gift To America

Once upon a time,
a hundred years ago,
there was a tiny little island,
which sat in the middle of a great big harbor.

Everyday, big boats from all over the world
sailed into the harbor,
right past the little island.

Many of the boats were filled with families
who were moving to a strange, new country called America.

Many families who sailed through the big harbor
and past the little island
were coming to live

in New York City.

Auguste Bartholdi

It was a beautiful spring morning in May, 1871,
when a large boat from France slowly sailed past
the tiny little island
in the middle of the great big harbor.
Auguste Bartholdi, a young French artist,
quickly put his paints and brushes away.

Safely tucked away in his suitcase was a painting.
This was Bartholdi's painting.

Bartholdi had a gift for America.

Soon after Bartholdi arrived in New York City, he decided to make a clay statue from his painting.

"This statue is not quite what I had in mind," he thought.

So, he made another one, and then another. At last, Bartholdi was happy. "This little brown statue is very beautiful, but maybe I should try to make her a little bigger."

And that's exactly what he did.
Back home in France,
Bartholdi started to build
a BIG STATUE. It was 1875.

"First, we'll build the hand that holds the torch."

Some twenty men hammered, while others plastered.
At night, the workers went home with white dust in their hair and on their faces.
Here's the hand and the torch being built.

One year later, the hammering stopped.
The copper hand and the torch were finished.
It was 1876.

Bartholdi took the hand and the torch
to a big fair in Philadelphia.

Inside the hand was a narrow little stairway.
Bartholdi climbed the stairs, around and around,
until he reached the torch.
Bartholdi could see the whole fair and
everyone at the fair could see —— Bartholdi!

When Bartholdi returned home to Paris, work began on the head and the crown.

Two years later, the workers laid their hammers down. The big shiny head and crown were finished. Bartholdi looked up at the statue's face and smiled. He had never seen anything so BIG in his entire life.

"Well, gentlemen, we're off to another fair! Thank heavens, it's in Paris this time." It was 1878.

Gustave Eiffel

Meanwhile, work on the statue continued.
Gustave Eiffel, a famous bridge builder,
was now helping Bartholdi.

"When we have a storm, I don't want her to blow
away," Bartholdi explained to Eiffel.
"And what if lightning should strike her?
I certainly don't want her to get hurt."

Gustave Eiffel laughed. "She'll last a long time, Bartholdi.
We make a good team. You just build the statue. I'll make her strong."

So, Gustave Eiffel and his men built an iron frame.
The frame was strong enough to hold the statue together.

After the Paris fair was over, the head and the crown were left
outside, next to the iron frame.

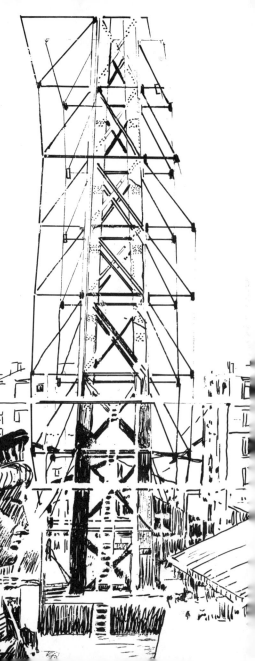

Slowly and carefully, the statue grew.

One hot summer's day,
Bartholdi ate a picnic lunch
right above the statue's knee.
It was 1883.

Everyday, she was getting bigger and
stronger, until one day,
the statue had outgrown even the
tallest houses in all of Paris.

And there she stood, very quietly,
for a long, long time.
She waited a whole year before
leaving Paris. It was 1885.

"Even if you aren't rich, please give something.
The pedestal must be finished."

People all over America read
Joseph Pulitzer's newspaper.
Suddenly, grown-ups and children understood.
The statue was a gift for everyone in America!

In New York City, people even put money for the
pedestal into boxes on the street.

Meantime… in America,
a pedestal was being built
for the statue to stand on.
When money ran out, work on
the pedestal stopped.

"This can't happen!"

Joseph Pulitzer made up his mind to do
something fast. Pulitzer wrote about the statue
and the pedestal in his newspaper. Joseph
Pulitzer asked everyone in America
to give a few pennies.

When the three French ships slowly sailed into New York Harbor,
crowds of people began to cheer. French flags flew; American flags waved.

"The statue's here! The statue's here!"
"She's on that boat!" The shouts echoed across the water.

"I don't see anything, do you?"
"She's all packed up in those wooden boxes, don't you see?"
It was June, 1885. The pedestal wasn't finished.

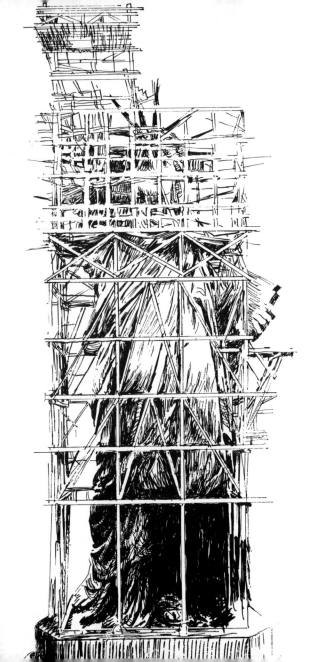

Two months later, work on the pedestal began again.
It was August, 1885.
At last, the statue would have a pedestal to stand on!

Nine months later, the pedestal was ready.
It was time to put the statue back together again.

Day after day, week after week,
every part fit together like a giant puzzle.

When the last two parts of the statue were finally put together,
workers quickly covered the statue's face with an
extra-large French flag. No one could see her face
until the big celebration.
Even Bartholdi would have to wait until October 28, 1886.

Even though it was a cold, rainy day in New York,
one million children and grown-ups lined the streets
for a very special parade.
Favorite French and American songs were played
by marching bands.
Red, white and blue flags of each country flew against a
gray sky. Excited hands waved to Auguste Bartholdi and
to Grover Cleveland, President of the United States.

After working for so many years, the day had arrived when Bartholdi would pull the rope that held the flag that covered the face of
THE STATUE OF LIBERTY

hrough the fog, Bartholdi heard the cheers.
ree hundred boats bobbed up and down in the
eat harbor, tooting their horns and
owing their whistles.

e statue was at home at last.
here on a tiny little island,
the middle of a great big harbor,
e torch was lit.

The very next day,
Liberty's light welcomed a boat full of families
who were coming to live in America.

Year after year, Liberty's light glowed
for thousands of others who followed.
Liberty watched as New York City grew.

Things were changing all the time.
In fact, seagulls were even changing.
In September, 1909, Liberty saw
a strange, noisy, new seagull fly right past
her torch. It was called an aeroplane.

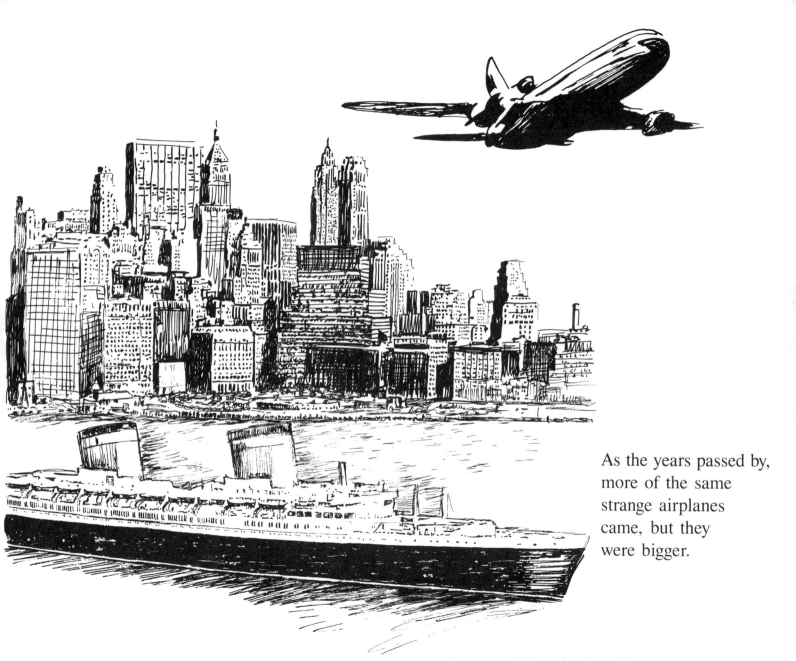

As the years passed by, more of the same strange airplanes came, but they were bigger.

Liberty's light kept right on shining, as the city grew taller and brighter

and taller again.

But to this very day, we are still reminded that her light keeps shining for each of us.

"The torch has been passed to a
new generation of Americans."*

*John F. Kennedy, Inaugural Address,
 January 20, 1961.